consider the light

poems and stories by

Kathi Crawford

Finishing Line Press
Georgetown, Kentucky

consider the light

ACKNOWLEDGMENTS

Thank you to the editors of the following publications, where selected poems first appeared,
sometimes in slightly different forms:

Blame it on the Heat Dome, *The Bayou Review,* Fall 2023 Edition
Ceilings, *Drunk Monkeys*
Chateau Couchebout, *Panoply, A Literary Zine*, Winter 2024 issue
Family Portrait, *ONE ART*: a journal of poetry
Flesh and Bone, *Ephemeral Elegies*
Ghosts of the Forest, *Flash Frontier* MANU | BIRD issue
Golden Bars, *Imposter Lit*, Volume 3, Issue I, Spring/Summer 2023
Grief, *Equinox* Volume 5, Fall 2023: Into the Thicket (hotpoet.org)
Notes on the 21st Century, Readings of a Seashore, and Reality, *The Write Launch,* Issue 74, June 2023
Self-Portrait as Make-Believe, *Full House Literary*, Spring Issue 1, 2024

My deepest gratitude to the many teachers and first readers for their continuing support, critique, and
encouragement of my writing practice. A special thank you to Kendra Preston Leonard for inspiring
this collection in the workshop she led for Writespace Houston, Cait Weiss Orcutt for her generous
nurturing, support, and feedback, and Kathryn Kulpa who helped me further hone and edit the
manuscript as part of a workshop she led.

A huge thank you to Brooke Summers-Perry, artist, writer, and facilitator of expressive and
compassionate life skills, whose artwork graces the cover of this book, inspired by my poem, "Being a
Cog in the Wheel of this Economic Engine." We submitted the poem and artwork for the 2024 WiVLA
(Women in the Visual and Literary Arts) collaboration project.

Much gratitude to Melody Locke, a traditional and alternative fine-art photographer, whose photo,
"Rest Stop," inspired the poem of the same name in this collection.

A special thank you to the readers of this book for your time and consideration of my work.

Publisher: Leah Huete de Maines
Editor: Christen Kincaid
Cover Art: Brooke Summers-Perry
Author Photo: Brittney M. Gomez, Brit Fine Photography
Cover Design: Elizabeth Maines McCleavy

Order online: www.finishinglinepress.com
            also available on amazon.com

Author inquiries and mail orders:
Finishing Line Press
PO Box 1626
Georgetown, Kentucky 40324
USA

Contents

Golden Bars

Preheat the oven—line a baking dish with pre-cut parchment paper. It's the easiest to use. If you don't know how to bake, no need to worry, lovely one. This recipe is easy. Just follow the instructions. Pretend I am your grandmother who knows the secret to a simple life. When I was a girl, I used my Easy Bake Oven to make cookies for my brothers. I learned how to be sweet and welcomed into a brood of men.

So, you'll need a mixing bowl and a large, wooden spoon. Beat the liquids together first then fold in the dry. This is a trick of the best bakers. There are things most men will never know. To make cookie bars, one way is the only way, but not in life. You can learn how to bake. You are from a long line of hardy women.

Pour the mixture into the dish. Smell the sugar as the bars turn golden. Pull the dish out of the oven at just the right moment. Set aside to cool. Don't touch the hot edges with your hands. Don't say yes to marrying someone you know is not the one. Hightail it out of there if it doesn't feel right. When the lies keep coming, it's time to go.

Pull out a fresh plate. Fill a glass of milk. You know what love is. This is just another way to learn how to survive.

Family Portrait

We stood a crooked line across the porch—
our father at the mill;
our mother held the camera.

She carefully arranged us for our annual photo session;
dressed me, the only girl, in all-white overalls,
laced-up shoes.

She staged a picture-pattern portrait each year;
light colors for me and dark for my brothers.

The two of us younger kids always clustered
around our second oldest brother knowing
the way he protected the ones he loved.

The oldest gazed away from the camera—
from my mother's eyes—
detached.

She held these zigzag-cut snapshots
with glue and photo corners
in her motherhood scrapbook—

until the fifth, another boy, was born.

After my parents divorced,
the anthology of our family

was found in a dresser drawer;
pictures scattered—

the context and timeline
ripped apart.

Rest Stop

Wild weeds and grass shoot up
between busted pavements.

Two gas pumps encircle the last century.
One askew; the other not.

Rain-soaked trees climb around the station.
Guard the muted storefront.

This block was once a hubbub of connection.
Now it is empty and overgrown.

As long as there are seeds, roots, and soil,
nature restores itself, dismantling constructions;

but not the memories.

Here, laughter poured from men, like my dad,
who smoked Marlboros and drank stale coffee

before the next shift.

Their children bloomed here,
imagining escape.

A Protest

It seems to me my mother breathed
a sigh of relief in the delivery room
when I emerged
a girl after a trio of boys in a time
of protests, the year disposable diapers
were created, and women
went to work.

As the only girl, the weight
of her expectations landed on me that day
and over time, collapsed
into my own protest
against the mold, a seed
that never touched
the ground.

Self-Portrait as Make-Believe

When I was five or six
my bedroom blossomed
with what my mother called
the pretending people.

        Like a linchpin   slipped
        through the axle of   a wheel
        they must have   held me

as flour binds
a tough cookie
protecting
the softness inside.

Flesh and Bone

It is said mothers raise daughters,
love sons.

You believed I could be contained.

Instead, I emerged a woman
bawling and bellowing,
a brown bear
raised on her hind legs,
fingers clawed.

Roller Skates, 1976

Swapping your soles with wheels,
you roar into the rink. Beast mode.
Gloria Gaynor belting *I Will Survive* vibes your rhythm.
You glide. You bounce. You roll along to *Ebony Eyes*.

But rolling along in front of you is the boy
you are crushing on crushing
on his latest girlfriend. Your pace slows
as panic presses against passion pulsing.

Three years later, you will find yourself in the back of his van
having sex for the first time. If you had known
this was how it would go down,
you would have rolled away.

But you didn't. You don't.
You can't let go of the desire
of your imagination. You don't yet know
it could happen any other way.

Graduation

My friends pile into the Ford
as I parade us around our high school grounds
dragging on a menthol cigarette.

As if we would be there together, rebels forever,
grooving, sipping Miller High Life, suspended
in time.

We belt out "Heartache Tonight"
with Don, Glenn, Bob, & J.D.; their last album
before the breakup comes.

Rusted factories & dismal prospects
our backdrop; the aching freedom
of leaving our closeness behind.

Let's Take a Ride

#1—Mercury Switch

The sunny, wide-open, blue sky captured me immediately as I pulled my brand new, cherry red, Toyota Corolla hatchback into a Houston, Texas Motel 6 parking lot in October 1980. I'd escaped the gray, cloudy, closed-in skies of Ohio two days before. At 19, with $500 in my pocket and a car payment due, I was like many others who left the Rust Belt for work in Bayou City.

After settling into an apartment and a new job, I joined a co-worker at Van's Stampede Ballroom on a Friday night. It was the era of urban cowboys and Houston offered an active country western dance scene. We ordered a drink at the bar and watched as couples two-stepped. My co-worker was approached by Greg, who told her he recently arrived from Kentucky. He asked her to dance. Not exactly her "John Travolta," she ditched him right after the song was over. He sulked onto the bar stool next to me. We talked into the night and ended up in my apartment.

Within weeks, we decided it was cheaper to live together, so he moved in. Over the months that followed, we fell in love. One weekend, he flew to Kentucky to visit family. He left me the keys to his black, Chevy Camaro Z28 in case I needed it.

#2—Muffler

Early Saturday afternoon, as I was walking into my building after running an errand, Joe, the man who lived in the apartment below us, approached me. He asked if I could give him a ride to his friend's house. I didn't really know Joe, but I had seen Greg talking to him in the parking lot from time to time. Impulsively, with small-town graciousness, I responded, "Yeah, sure, I can take you." We agreed to leave later in the afternoon.

When we met up, Joe was carrying a large, black, gym bag. As we approached the Camaro, Joe said firmly, "I'll drive." Because of his aggressive tone, I nodded my head, gave him the keys, and got in the passenger seat. He threw his bag in the back seat, and we left. Shortly after, he pulled into a convenience store and picked up a man who was standing outside. I moved to the back seat and sat next to Joe's bag. It was unzipped. I peeked inside and saw what looked like switchblade knives with the blades flicked open—sharp and glinting from the sun as it inched its way below the horizon.

Joe handed me a Quaalude. I took it and chugged it down with a beer. Maybe I thought it would calm my nerves by doing so. I tried to pay attention to where we were going. I still didn't know how to get around the city. I noticed we were on Highway 45 heading north. It seemed like we were in the car forever as the sun went down and the moon rose. Finally, Joe pulled off the highway into a parking lot.

As we got out of the car, Joe took his bag out of the back. We walked to his friend's apartment, and the man who opened the door let us in. Joe exchanged an envelope with his friend and sat down next to me on the couch. He kept looking over at me, put his arm around me, and kept handing me beers. He and his friend talked for hours. The man who rode there with us left. The friend asked if he could hitch a ride back to town with us. Joe said, "Sure" as if he owned the car he was driving. He picked up his bag and we all got in the car.

I drank more beers as my mind worked on how I was going to get myself out of this. I knew those knives were in the bag and I was in a car headed to my apartment with two men I did not know. It was after midnight, and we were less than a mile from home when Joe's friend said, "I'm hungry." Joe pulled into an all-night diner around the corner from our apartment building. We went inside and sat down. I ordered a Margarita. I tried to stay calm. My drink was gone in two gulps.

This part of the story is a bit of a mystery to me. The diner was packed with people including a table of cops. I was told that I passed out in front of everyone and rolled off my chair onto the floor. I woke up as the cops shoved Joe and his friend into chairs in a back room. One cop pulled me outside. He read me the riot act for getting mixed up with a drug dealer. As he drove me to my apartment, he said, "You're lucky to be alive!"

#3—Mirror

On Sunday afternoon, Greg flew back from Kentucky. I picked him up at the airport in my car, since the Camaro had been towed the night before, and shared the play-by-play.

"I thought Joe was your friend," I said.

"That guy was never my friend! I was only nice to him because, when I went to his place to buy a dime bag, I saw blood stains all over his walls and knew he was dangerous. I didn't want to tick him off!"

I realized at this moment that my body intervened for me when I fainted in the restaurant.

Luckily, Joe never returned to the apartment and this small-town girl learned a big-town lesson.

Constructive Criticism

Don't take anything personally.

Don't listen to the stranger who says you're too loud.
Don't disagree when your boss criticizes your work.
Don't believe your friend when she says you're wrong.
Don't trust your mother when she says she's starting a new life
because she didn't like the last one.

Remember, it's not about you. Otherwise,
words may alter you; set you up to suffer.

Nothing others say or do is yours.

You are only hearing *their* longings,

their outrage,

their dreams.

Don't make it about you.

Someone in Little River, California, Is Aching for Love
after Alex Dimitrov

This poem is happening
in a cliffside cottage
on the Mendocino Coast
where the cadence of waves
crashing against the edge
are so melodious it's impossible
to stay inside. The midday sun breaks
through early morning clouds
while I watch. Every morning
I sip my coffee
and consider the reasons
I said *yes* to this rendezvous.
A match made to a man
I did not know.
Hello, strange man I'll never want
to see again. No *Same Time,*
Next Year for us.
Are we all lost, even when
the deep blue waters of the Pacific Ocean
are looking up at us?
In this post-break-up, pre-now, situation
I was breaking all *The Rules.*
This place, this strange
man, even shorebirds digging
in the sand could not take my mind
off of a kind of love I know exists
but do not have.
Hello, fellow resort couples
walking hand-in-hand
on the rocky shore. Hello, you two
cliff-side tenderly
looking into one another's eyes.
The lights turn on. Dusk settles.
Someone in a cliffside cottage
in Little River, California
is aching for love.

For the Love of Cleaning

When I decided to continue my studies at Richland Community College in my early twenties, I moved in with a friend to save money. We set ground rules: the only room allowed to be messy was her bedroom; the common areas were to be kept clean; and we would thoroughly clean the apartment together once a week. I soon discovered that her idea of "keeping the common areas clean" was not the same as mine. Often, after a long day of work and school, as I walked through the front door of our apartment, I would hear the sound of roaches racing away from the light. As I glanced into the kitchen, the smell of bacteria lifted up from the dirty dishes in the sink. In the living room, half-eaten Taco Bell nachos sat in their take-a-way box on the coffee table. Down the hallway to the door of my roommate's bedroom lay a trail of clothes. Inside I knew she was in bed sound asleep. I would move into action and clean up the mess.

My discipline for cleaning developed early. Our home felt chaotic to me. Cleaning was a way for me to gain a sense of control. As I moved through a room, my mind calmed and my mood lifted. When everything is in its place and a room takes on the fresh smell of cleaning products, I feel a sense of accomplishment and bliss. I believe as the Buddhists do—how you act in small ways is how you act in big ways. Taking care of my home is a reflection of who I am and how I take care of myself and my family.

Growing up, we visited Nanna in Pennsylvania multiple times a year. I loved the fresh, antiseptic smell as we walked in the door. Nanna's orderly home was a constant comfort to me. Her attention to what was going on in my life made me feel seen. I liked to help her in the kitchen as she cooked. My stomach would rumble as the chicken roasted in the oven, the potatoes boiled on the stove, and the moist, chocolatey, cake made from scratch, with thick layers of chocolate icing, sat on the counter. After dinner, we washed dishes together. My time with Nanna was so different than my experience at home. As latchkey kids, during the week, we cooked dinner on our own while Mom worked late, and Dad worked at the mill.

Nanna wrote to me often after I moved to Houston. She knew I was alone and that I didn't know anyone there. The first letter she sent me offered advice: "Kathi, I know you will probably get lonely and homesick but if you get a nice job with a good future, just stick it out. Things will get better as time goes by. Now that you are on your own, take a little advice from an old woman. If you find some nice boy down there and feel you have to have sex with him, for heaven's sake, get on the "pill" so you don't have an unwanted child. You are too young to be tied down yet. You know they did not have the "pill" when I was young or your mother. So be a good girl and try to see it my way." She finished the letter with, "How is your cooking? Ha! Ha!."

I took Nanna's advice.

Now, when I open Nanna's Betty Crocker cookbook, I follow her notes in the margins and make the adjustments she made to the recipes. In the process of cooking, I can still catch her reflection off the gleam of the stove and hear her voice in my ear nudging me along my life's journey.

Self-Portrait at Twenty-Five

It's all late nights at the executive oak desk given to you for free by your past employer, a desk as heavy as your course load. It's the three-year grind you signed up for—the value of a college education to pull you out of the working class.

It's all creative financing. It's saying "no" to money from your family. It's okay to live with them, to accept food and clothing, but not money. Self-funded—how you will know you did it yourself.

It's all showtime that first day of the fall semester, walking into class knowing it's non-traditional to be Kathi Lynn Crawford (one of three students over the average age of 22.5). It's your dad in your ear, "I'm so proud of you. Don't give up."

It's all Madonna's big perm, neon blue shirt, over-sized leather jacket, high-waisted jeans tucked into snow boots stomping across campus. It's the dank smell of ice melting, bare trees, and sky.

It's nature's shifting seasons as you work and study with no respite. It's study time all the time. It's heavy books in your backpack, writing longhand, researching at the library.

It's realizing you live in a mecca for music; maybe you should find time to listen. It's Michael Stanley at the Agora serenading Cleveland with "My Town." It's Joe Walsh at the KSU Memorial Gym singing "Life's Been Good."

It's nights at JB's on Water Street pretending to be free enough to dance and drink the night away, books and bills be damned. It's a dalliance with a younger man picked up at the bar.

It's forgetting your false start, post-high school, Texas move for work—before this. It's leaving behind this sad, cold, Ohio life. It's grinding through the finish line, to a future you believe will be better, must be better.

Seasonal Disruptions

My parents argued at the top of the stairs—
the echo of their words deepening
the bitter cold of winter. I strain to hear, pressed
behind my bedroom door. I was eight years old
and knew by then, I hate winter. The shedding
of the leaves, the snow-covered ground,
shorter days, longer nights, four of us in school,
a baby at home, and dad working shifts.
Is it worth getting married and having children
only to find yourself struggling to make
ends meet? I cannot answer.
I was too young to even consider the question.
I need to save my family. Here now,
I wash and fold clothes, clean up after meals,
and watch my baby brother
when mom works late. Then, older, I won't
follow in her footsteps. I wanted to live
before I got married. But the pressure grew.
Later, in college in my late 20s, I dated someone
who lived in the house he and his ex-girlfriend bought.
She lived there too. I married him before I knew
the extent of my mistake.
Three years later, winter again. I found myself lying
on our carpeted bathroom floor. Ends unmet.
How can we know we are doing the right thing?
By spring I took flight. Pursued renewal.
The deep, darkening winter
is a time of shedding. *The right thing becomes*
whatever you have to do.

Readings of a Seashore

1
Looking at Jessie Buckley's red hair
you notice the sunset scattering the light.
which is what happens when you look at Jessie Buckley's hair.
Always the same thing: the stunning sunset,
the crest and break of ocean waves
like the musical notes of her brogue.

2
But looking into the eyes of Olivia Coleman
is like looking into the eyes of a falling tide.
Did you know that tides
are not higher or lower at night
as the moon's pull is not stronger than the earth's?
Nothing controls the tide or Olivia Coleman
except for depression.

At the seashore, you notice a raft
amongst the seashells on the tidal flat. You listen
to the rhythm of seamen raking
fish, crabs, mussels, and clams
from the brackish water. You settle.

3
In either case, soon you are in your brother's apartment,
which is not important. What is important is to ignore
his raging, beer-sodden voice
reverberating in your ears;

the force of the ebb
pulling through your body.

Ode to Leaving My Apartment

I want to leave their arguments, late-night parties,
& TVs blaring at 4 a.m. I want my walls

to be surrounded by Southern magnolia trees,
tomatoes, basil, & cucumbers planted lovingly by me.

I want to live away from the tracks.
Somewhere where the train whistle won't blow

in the middle of the night. I don't wanna
have to say *good morning* to the neighbor;

the one whose headboard banged
against my wall for hours the night before.

I tried to create comfort inside
a constrained space & failed.

Let me root down in a refuge with my love
once we find a place to own.

No way you'd be able to
get me to leave.

Nesting Doll

It was high noon the day Sonya and I sat across from each other at La Madeleine. Our only connection was my ex-husband, Jeff, who married Sonya soon after our divorce ten years before. My intention was to never be involved with him again, but here I was, meeting with his wife after she reached out to me on Facebook. Perhaps it was the undertone of desperation I noticed in her message that gave me the sense she felt I was the only one who might validate her decision to leave him.

The restaurant was not too crowded, and we had the outside patio to ourselves. We hadn't met each other before and the purpose of Sonya reaching out to me brought us together a bit awkwardly. She thanked me for agreeing to meet. I said, "Of course," then asked, "What's going on?" Sonya shared that she had moved out of the house with her boys and was staying with a friend. Jeff didn't know where they were, but he had frozen their bank accounts.

Sitting on that patio in the sun, I watched as tears welled up in her eyes. I could hear the anxiety in her voice and in the way she kept looking around as if he might just show up. I felt compassion for the situation she was in, and, at the same time, a sigh of relief for escaping the grip of his manipulations.

"I'm so sorry, Sonya," I said, "I had to escape too. Except, when I moved out, I had a job, a separate bank account, and no children to worry about.

Sonya, unable to listen, interrupted, "I think I'm going crazy." I heard the edginess in her voice and decided to share my story with her to ease her stress and try to help her understand she was not the crazy one.

"He lied to me too. Early in our marriage, I was on the road a lot for my job. One day after returning from a trip, our neighbor was in our kitchen talking with Jeff about a home security business they started together that I knew nothing about. Shortly after, he was fired from his job because he was running this business when he was supposed to be working. I should have left him then, but he convinced me it was the direction he wanted to take in his career, and he begged me for forgiveness for not telling me about it. Later I found out he lost his life savings in the business and didn't pay our taxes. I left and filed for divorce."

With a faraway look in her eyes and sadness in her voice, Sonya said, "Yes, my relationship with him has turned into a mess of mind games. When we first met, he was extremely devoted and loving. I couldn't believe my good fortune."

"Like a dream come true," I interjected. "It's amazing how quickly the dream turns into a nightmare with Jeff."

Sonya was learning he was like a nesting doll wherein each doll inside each doll reveals another doll until the "secret" is found inside the last doll. Inside Jeff, it turns out, is a heart of stone.

We sat in silence. I picked up the check and we left.

Ceilings

At first it was easy to tell
myself the story about limits—women
don't work, we find a man, get married,
have babies—and if we do work
it doesn't mean we'll be paid
a living wage because we don't
have a family to provide for and we can't
live in the city all by ourselves
because it's dangerous—and on and on
it goes but even then—I'm still trying
to clear the runway of my life
reaching for what was always
there for me except for

my belief in ceilings
you see the world wants you
to believe there are limits
you cannot break through
as a way to control you
yet this barrier is not real
it's imagined because there really
are no limits—only in your mind
where your inner critic lives—

in fact, to live this empowered lifestyle,
traditional gender tropes must be
dismantled yet research reveals
that men find less powerful women
attractive and I always say
"atta girl" because people like
when the underdog wins.

Being a Cog in the Wheel of this Economic Engine

makes me feel like I am lost in life. Being anywhere makes me gasp for air.
Each day I begin with the hope for energy to fuel my spirit as I forge
through capitalist expectations to buy my continued existence.

If I am the fuel mixing with air, why am I not ignited?
Where is the spark plug to connect me with myself?
I need to find compassion for the me that lives inside the me that lives on
the outside.
Each day I wake conscious of my quandary, and it distracts me.
My halting efforts toward artistic expression are rooted in the belief,
"Hard work is good for the soul!"

In Self-Portrait with Thorn Necklace and Hummingbird,
courage fumes out of Frida Kahlo's fixed gaze.
The essence of who we are flames—
stroke by stroke on a canvas, line by line on the page, plant by plant in the
dirt.

Self-Portrait as Riding Shotgun

Remembering my last road trip with Dad in his purple pickup truck the color of "Barney."

Dad comfortable behind the wheel. He refused to fly on a plane.

He was in charge and would not let me drive.

We adventured the first time for a 36-hour drive when I turned 19 and moved south.

Dad drove shotgun behind my car, guarding me in transit, making sure I arrived safely.

This time I rode shotgun next to my dad, now 70, keeping an eye out for dangerous conditions as focused as a polar bear protecting her cub.

I am not a girly girl. I am my daddy's girl. Outcasts of our family of seven. Two one-of-a-kinds like the color purple. Not primary hues. More independent. Awarded our own kind of purple heart for bravery.

We didn't know this would be Dad's last road trip to Texas. Not because he didn't want to make the drive every year, but because I didn't want him driving alone.

After four hours, we had not stopped.

Nor would we.

Except for gas or a nap by the side of the road.

I was required to hold it until we stopped.

I sat straight up with good posture and good humor and engaged in lively debate to keep him awake.

I pestered him to check into a motel for sleep and a shower.

Finally, we stopped in Memphis and stayed at the Relax Inn. Back on the road before sunrise.

In the early morning hours, Dad pulled into a gas station in a part of a town we did not know.

He casually strode in and out of the store to pay the cashier as I held my breath.

Anything could happen to him. Even then, I knew how precious this moment in time was to me.

Reality

Not reality television, with sculpted
scenarios and tired trysts, but a prickly pear cactus
that stores drops of water in its pads,
astute at adapting in excessive climatic conditions.

I know how it feels to be a survivor in a desert,
the unending corporate climb,
the evaporating promise of upward mobility.
I wish life were as easy as it seems to be

for the virtual nobodies
turned on by a momager exploiting
her children for fame, manipulating
family and fan ratings.

I, too, make fruit out of nothing.

Reality is a sharp morsel
of moisture in a land
with sparse water.

Notes on the 21st Century

It's not the end of the world, though it could be, but the sun
came up today and I've had my morning coffee, while, at the same time,
Yellowstone stood rain-smothered, the Midwest roiled in the midst of a
heat wave,
and millions across India and Bangladesh lost everything to raging floods
and landslides.
I mean, every day beats me down as I suffer in this Texas heat—
though maybe not completely down. I find strength in my lover's bear hug,
the steady voice of my niece, and lavender flowering in my backyard.
Everyday people are murdered by guns, by laws, by climate emergencies; as
my brain struggles
to understand why the persistent focus is on hurting each other. We are
shrinking
the spaces capable of being lived in, driving
ourselves to desperate acts of survival,
and, though I am looking for the bright side,
Mother Earth is eating her young,
and maybe the world ends here.

Grief

We sat in rusted lawn chairs. A black squirrel stared at us
        from the edge of the woods—such tiny surrender.
        A breeze cooled us—leaves of amber, auburn, and crimson drifted '
        to the ground.
        A residue lingered in the air from chain-smoked Marlboros—
        words failed. I left.

Negative space is the area around and between the subject of an image—
        it's the silence, the gutters, the margins, the space between
        columns.
        Grief and art are a process. If the person who died is the object of
        grief,
        the people around the object are taken off balance—
        now in the darkness, the quiet, the gap.

He stared at me through the plate glass window; beckoned me to stare back.
        As I descended the stairs, we held each other's gaze.
        It was the two-year anniversary of my brother's death.
        The blackbird's appearance surprised me.
        He brought me to a standstill, then he flew away.

In my dream, I shared memories with a friend who died the year before.
        She felt she disappointed me,
        but I was not disappointed—
        only her love remained in my heart.
        I awoke to the five-year anniversary of my brother's death.

On a spring day after the rain, my brother's three-year-old grandson
        rolled his tricycle through the mud over and over.
        His laughter emanated through the rustling leaves.
        The blackbird watched from the tree above.
        A whole scene unfolded in the negative space.

I Tried to Keep it Together During the Pandemic and Failed

like when my funding was pulled for college
       after I left my job and moved in with my brother;

or after securing a loan for said education
       when my car engine seized after an oil change;

by which I mean I kept it together, as we all do,
       by separating my emotions from each blow

like when I learned my ex-husband hadn't paid our taxes
       and left me on the hook.

I made myself get back up every time.

       Before my dad died.

              Then, I thought, okay, you win; I'll stay down.

On a Zoom call, a well-intentioned friend told me my dad could do so
much more for me
       now that he was free of his body.

       What the hell?

I missed Dad's laugh; how he would yell at the TV
       as if the newscaster could hear his arguments;

sleeping on the twin-sized bed at his house
       with my feet dangling off;

eating eggs and drinking coffee at his favorite diner,
       being together.

Have you ever released the ashes of someone you love?

Have you ever released—
             everything?

The Trouble with Bar Stools

Leg #1—1985

Jeanie sat on a high cushioned bar stool with her feet tucked underneath in deep conversation with the bartender at Nick's Uptown, the first stop on our bar crawl. Jeanie was my party partner. Her purse perched on the bar stool next to her as she awaited my arrival. She wore a creamy white, long-sleeved top and matching skirt. Her long, thick, blond hair was twisted atop her head. A pale Mexican lager sat in front of her on the bar top, the lime squeezed through the opening, leaving juice around the lip of the bottle. I waltzed up to her in my little black dress, took the seat, and ordered a Corona.

Leg #2—2021

The six of us gathered to celebrate our reunion after two years of being grounded by COVID. We relaxed and caught up in casual soliloquies. "We have something to tell you," Sue said suddenly after we clicked our champagne glasses to toast our friends visiting from Tennessee. The tone of her voice brought us to attention.

"We put a down payment on a life plan community and will be moving there in three years once it's built." She called it their DIP home. I learned DIP means dying in place. As I shared my congratulations, I felt anxiety halting my breath. I was just getting used to being sixty. When was the right time to consider dying in place?

Leg #3—2021

That night at Nick's Uptown I didn't know the nights of sitting on bar stools would end. Over the course of my life, I had transformed from teetering on three-legged bar stools to resting in a place of harmony, wisdom, and understanding. I was 25 when I returned to college to finish my degree at a time when most people that age had graduated from college and were starting careers and families. I was 30 when I first married, and in my haste to "catch up," I married the wrong person. At 38, I married the right person, too late for us to have or want children. Here I am, again, at 60, holding out for what is right for me, not yet ready to claim a DIP home.

Over the years, I lost touch with Jeanie and many other close friends. Grateful to have attracted these angels for a time or a season. Today, my collection of friends is like a grove of trees—rooted, life-giving relationships that have stood the test of time. We stand stronger than the bar stools of my youth; prepared to carry each other through our senior years.

Blame it on the Heat Dome

that I don't go outside
anymore; no daily walks
when it's 100+, sun
glaring, cement
storing heat, glasses
rolling down
my sweaty nose;
hair in a ponytail;
my boiled
brain no longer
Texas tough;
the planet is
warming, an
existential crisis
in full bloom;
like an armadillo
I burrow down;
my home an oasis;
a little, green
spot in the desert;
I lie depleted,
dormant in my bed
or laze
in my Relax
the Back Chair;
all the shades drawn,
I don't check
the temperature
knowing today
is a day
just like the day
before; too woozy
to wonder where
a livable space
might be
in a world
that is whirling.

Full of Holes

I imagine
the subtle squeezing
of my bones,
the dry carving
of tiny holes,
my skeleton
ripped apart
like a decomposed
sponge. I am
a dynamic creature
connected by
a structure
easily torn
by a silent thief
who whittles away
my bone tissue
into a perforated grid
until my spine
eventually crumbles
into its center.
I take what I can get
find ways to soothe
the aches and pains.
My spirit, penetrable
as a pocket of air,
bristles
at the doctor's
attitude of
there's-nothing-you-
can-do-about-it.
But I can do
something about it.
I can soak up
what's left of my life
until it's worn
to shreds.

Chateau Couchebout

I even love the Bernese
Mountain Dogs, Benz and Heidi,
was thinking this as I walked through the vines
with the vigneron
who prunes the shoots and clusters
to unblock the light
knowing the grapes
by the shape and texture
of their leaves—Merlot, Malbec,
Sauvignon, and Cabernet,
the Chateau windows
witnessing the field
a scene for Impressionists on canvas
later I was thinking I even like this outside patio
where we sit on tall bar stools
around the table, dine
on grilled duck, and nose the wines
twenty minutes from Bordeaux,
the fruit beginning to form
on the cusp of summer
I too am on the cusp
I feel the warmth of the sun
a slight breeze blows, and I remember
longing for this get-a-way,
delayed by a worldwide pandemic
forcing us to miss the French culture
the timing perhaps perfect after all
to chance an invitation
from the chef at a local restaurant,
the son of the Chateau's owner,
to be here with his family
the reason travel, and risking it,
is life.

Afternoons in the Test Kitchen

After you've cleared your schedule,
after you've set up your bowls, mixer, measuring cups, and spoons,
after you've pulled ingredients from your cabinets and fridge,
like America's Test Kitchen, this is where the magic happens.
Like Ina Garten, you are love drunk being in your home kitchen,
but, unlike a cooking competition, you must use a recipe
no matter how frequently you've made the dish.
Like when you lost your banana bread instructions
at your friend's house, where you stayed after Hurricane Ike,
the banana bread you'd been making for twenty years.
You could not re-create it without guidance.
Your friend continuously sent you banana bread recipes
asking—*Is this it? How about this one? This has to be it!*
Until years later, a picture of banana bread popped
into your Instagram feed from your favorite cook,
Tieghan Gerard. Though not the same bread,
it passed the test, soft enough
with lots of bananas, baking up perfectly.
The trick is if you find a dish you enjoy
after making it three or more times,
adjusting as you see fit, you will write a recipe card.
Add it to your collection.
And when your husband asks you to make his favorite
buttery lemon pasta with almonds and arugula,
you tell him, be warned,
it will take you longer than the recipe says. Longer
than you promised. Longer than you could imagine.
Similar to a long, drawn-out speech, kitchen time
is your "me" time. You are chef and sous chef
wrapped into one. It's all sauté, season, substitute,
savor, and sing. You taste how the flavors combine and say—
wasn't that easy?—
tuck away the card.

Ghosts of the Forest

You find them quietly perched on the edges of meadows or forest openings—nearly invisible—but when they hit you with their mesmerizing stare, their yellow eyes boring through, like human eyes in a feathered suit—it's like they know it's time for you to take a leap of faith.

In this stage of my life, windows and doors are closing, and I am searching for an opening—a way out. Like the time I was lost in the woods behind my childhood home. I was trying to find the creek alone because my brother wouldn't come with me. I was hell-bent on finding it. Lost, I franticly ran through the trees and brush to find the path to the backyard until, instead, the creek appeared, but at a different point along the water line. I sat on the edge catching my breath when my brother suddenly, quietly, appeared.

And now, the deep, booming hoot of the mysterious Strix nebulosa is calling me to clock out of corporate life, to trust the steps ahead. It's time to stop playing this soul-robbing game; to break through the hard-packed snow and forage what's beneath. I understand I am, as much as anyone, an endangered species seeking a way to live in the midst of impermanence. I can only hope to navigate this closing act of my life with the wingspan of the Great Grey Owl.

Trumbull County, Northeast Ohio, Age 16

Even though it's winter & I'm stuck inside most days,
somehow I manage to get out of bed, get dressed, & fed.
Even though I'd rather stay tucked in until spring arrives,
I venture out to my car for the evening shift. Packed in the trunk:
a sleeping bag, flashlight, first aid kit, food, water.
It's impossible to be prepared for everything, but just in case,
I feel ready. At my drive-thru station a woman rolls in to get her coffee
& Egg McMuffin. She tells me, "It's not hard to survive
if you bundle up and let a good attitude keep you warm and fuzzy."
Somehow I manage a pleasant, "Thank you," when I want to say, "Eat shit."
Even though I'd like to be on a beach, it's impossible to imagine paradise
from here.
That night as I crawl down Mahoning Avenue,
the walls of snow piled along both sides are no longer white.
They've turned into a gray & black-tinged dress of dirt.

I will escape this place someday.

And I will think, later, that it was worth this.

Growing up here, I mean.

Even now, there is a warm place, somehow,

somewhere, waiting for me.